JOBS IN SCIENCE

By Bethany Latham

KidHaven PUBLISHING

Published in 2026 by
KidHaven Publishing, an Imprint of
Greenhaven Publishing, LLC
2544 Clinton St., Buffalo, NY 14224

Written by: Bethany Latham
Edited by: Rebecca Phillips-Bartlett
Designed by: Rob Delph

Cataloging-in-Publication Data

Names: Latham, Bethany.
Title: Jobs in science / Bethany Latham.
Description: Buffalo, NY : KidHaven Publishing, 2026. | Series: STEAM job? Dream job! | Includes glossary and index.
Identifiers: ISBN 9781534552210 (pbk.) | ISBN 9781534552227 (library bound) | ISBN 9781534552234 (ebook)
Subjects: LCSH: Science--Vocational guidance--Juvenile literature.
Classification: LCC Q147.L384 2026 | DDC 502.3--dc23

Printed in China

CPSIA compliance information: Batch #QW26KH: For further information contact Greenhaven Publishing LLC at 1-844-317-7404.

Please visit our website, www.greenhavenpublishing.com.
For a free color catalog of all our high-quality books, call toll free 1-844-317-7404 or fax 1-844-317-7405.

Find us on

IMAGE CREDITS

Images courtesy of Shutterstock.com, unless otherwise stated.

Cover – Stock-Asso, Vadim Almiev. 4–5 – Gorodenkoff, Frame Stock Footage, KlingSup, ShadeDesign, DimaBerlin, TetianaKtv, Rashad Ashur, riabchevskii. 6–7 – Gorodenkoff, Shaiith, afotostock, Mila Drumeva, riabchevskii. 8–9 – ORION PRODUCTION, kimman, Nuva Frames. 10–11 – PeopleImages.com – Yuri A, D.L.Rybalchenko, Drazen Zigic. 12–13 – seahorsetwo, Rashad Ashur, Elnur. 14–15 – tilialucida, riabchevskii, PeopleImages.com – Yuri A. 16–17 – PeopleImages.com – Yuri A, ShadeDesign, Rawpixel.com. 18–19 – tilialucida, Gorodenkoff, Achmad Yuge. 20–21 – Chutima Chaochaiya, GoodStudio, Olena Yakobchuk. 22–23 – Asier Romero, riabchevskii, PeopleImages.com – Yuri A. 24 – Achmad Yuge, riabchevskii. Vectors used throughout – Vadim Almiev, YamabikaY.

CONTENTS

Words that look like **this** can be found in the glossary on page 24.

ALL ABOUT STEAM

Have you ever thought about what you want to do when you grow up? There are many different **careers**. STEAM careers use science, technology, engineering, the arts, and math.

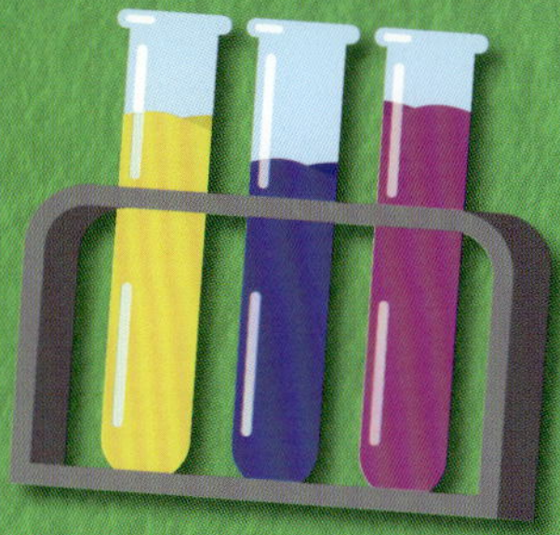

STEAM subjects are often linked. The skills you learn in one STEAM subject can help you in another. The things you learn in school can help you in many amazing STEAM careers.

ALL ABOUT SCIENCE

Science is the study of the world around us. This includes **natural** and human-made things. Science helps us understand how things work.

SCIENCE IS SPLIT INTO DIFFERENT AREAS, INCLUDING BIOLOGY, CHEMISTRY, AND PHYSICS.

Biology is the study of living things, such as plants.

Chemistry is the study of what things are made of.

Physics is the study of matter and energy, such as light and sound.

BE INSPIRED!

LET'S HAVE A LOOK AT SOME DREAM JOBS IN SCIENCE!

VET

Vets care for animals. They help them stay healthy and treat them when they are sick. Different vets look after different animals. These include pets, farm animals, and **exotic** animals, such as parrots.

THE FIRST VET SCHOOL WAS STARTED IN FRANCE IN 1761.

Vets use biology in their work. They need to know about animals and their bodies. Vets take special classes in college, which is a kind of school you can go to after high school.

DENTIST

Dentists are a type of doctor. They look after people's mouths and teeth. Dentists do many different things, including filling cavities, or tiny holes in teeth, checking people's teeth, and giving advice about brushing.

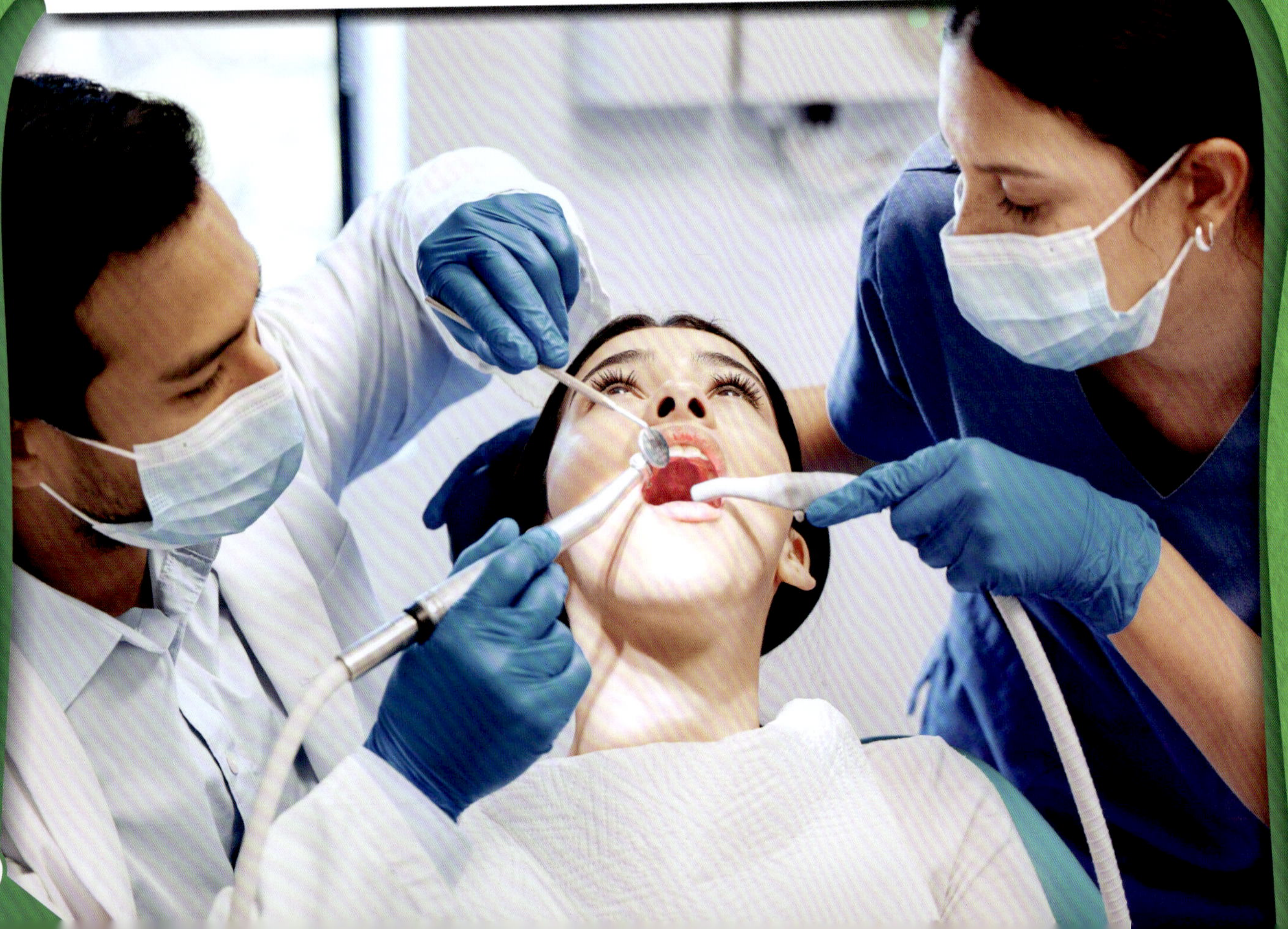

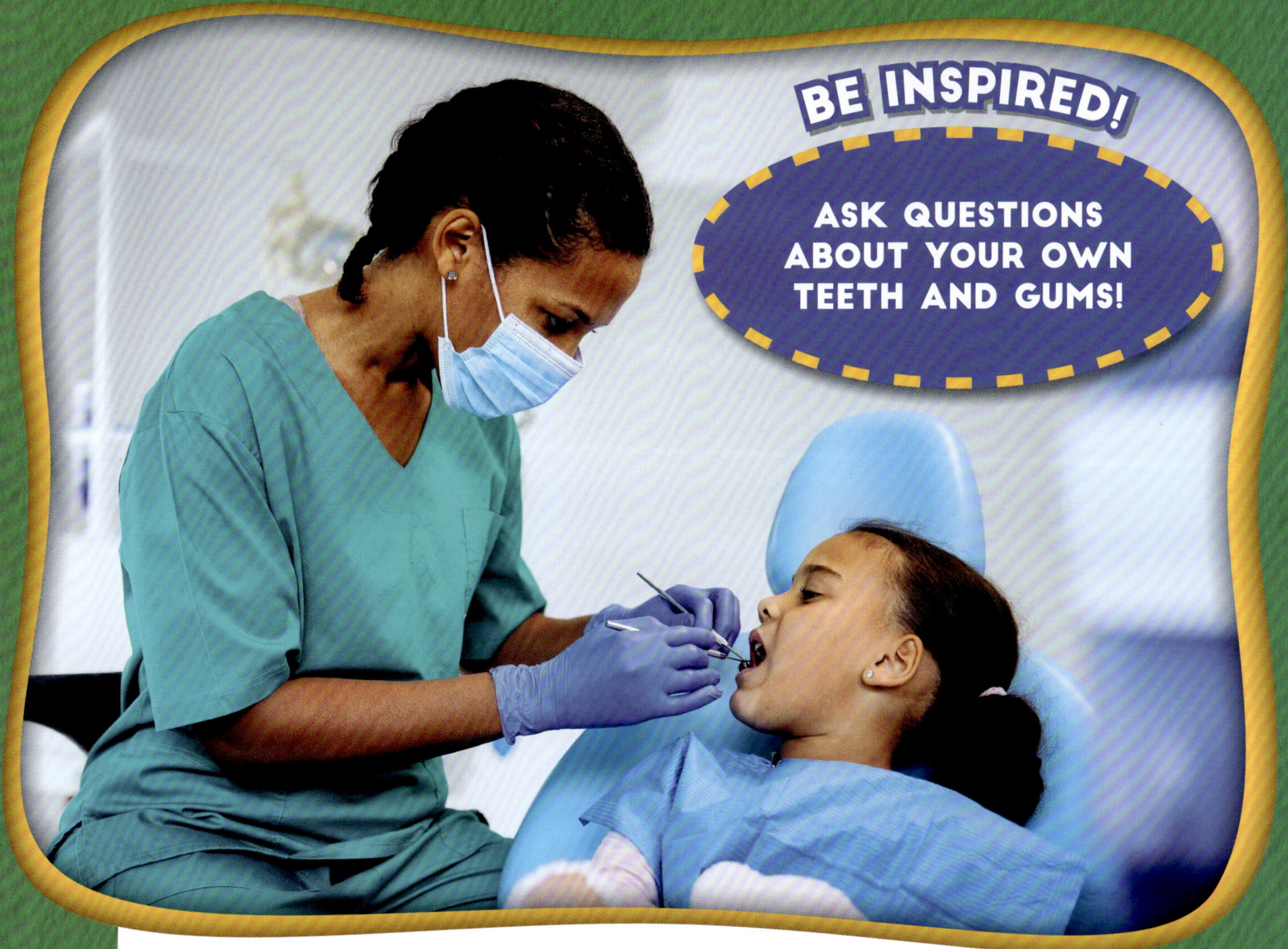

Dentists need to know about the human body and how it works. Dentists have to study for many years before they can begin working. Some dentists train for even longer and become **specialists**.

PHYSICIST

Physicists are scientists who study physics. There are two main types of physicists. Theoretical physicists use math to create **theories** about how things work. Experimental physicists do tests, or experiments, to explore how things work.

EXPERIMENTAL PHYSICISTS SOMETIMES DO EXPERIMENTS WITH LASERS.

Different physicists study different things, such as space or sound. They work to understand all they can about their subject. Physicists need good math skills and lots of **curiosity**.

LAB TECHNICIAN

Lab technicians work in laboratories. A laboratory is a place where scientists do research, tests, and experiments. Lab technicians run tests and record the results. They also take care of the **equipment**.

Lab technicians work in many different types of labs. These include medical laboratories and physics laboratories. Lab technicians need to know about science and math to do their job well.

NURSE

Nurses are medical workers. They care for people who are sick or hurt. Nurses often work in hospitals with doctors. Some nurses only treat children or older people. Other nurses visit sick people at home.

Nurses need to know many things about the human body. Usually, nurses go to nursing school after high school. Just like doctors, nurses can become specialists in many different things.

BE INSPIRED!

ASK QUESTIONS ABOUT HOW YOUR BODY WORKS.

EPIDEMIOLOGIST

Epidemiologists are scientists who study how diseases spread. They do **surveys** of sick and healthy people. Epidemiologists think of ways to keep people safe and stop them from getting sick. They sometimes work in hospitals.

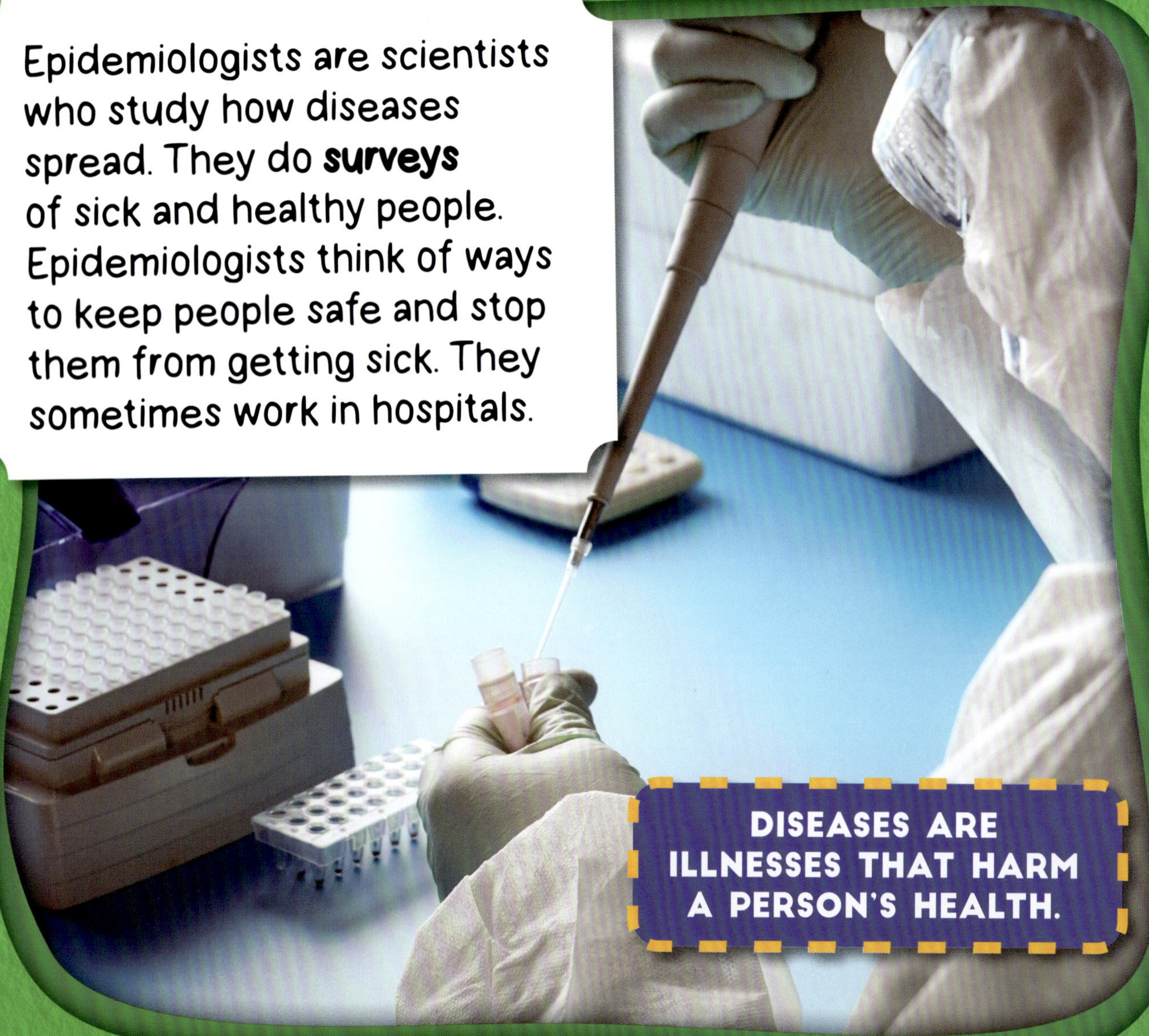

DISEASES ARE ILLNESSES THAT HARM A PERSON'S HEALTH.

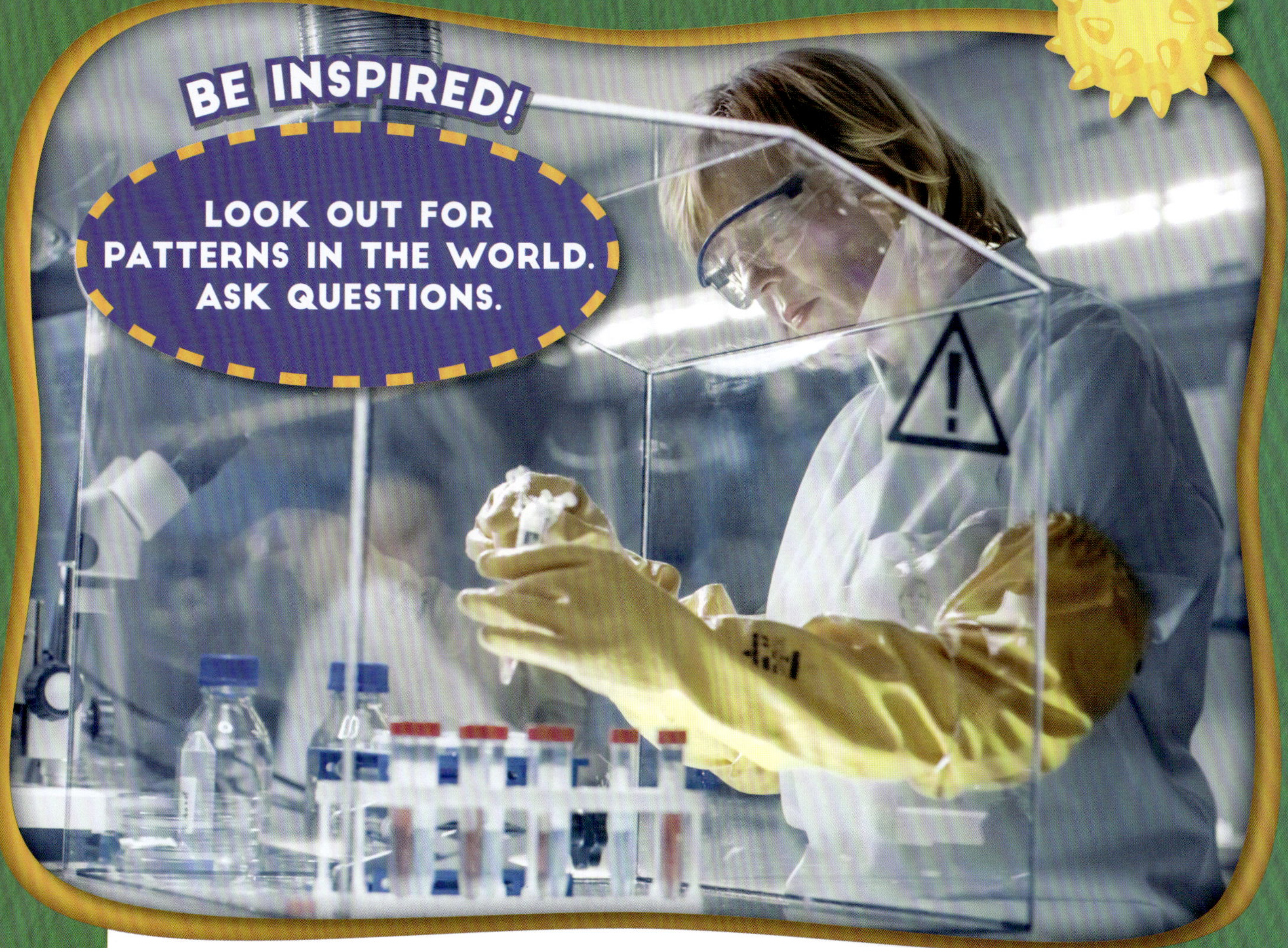

Epidemiologists need to know about biology and medicine to do their job well. Epidemiologists must study for a long time. They build up their skills and knowledge by doing special training after school.

MATERIALS SCIENTIST

Materials scientists study how different materials work. They create new materials to do certain jobs. Materials scientists work in many different areas, such as electronics and medicine.

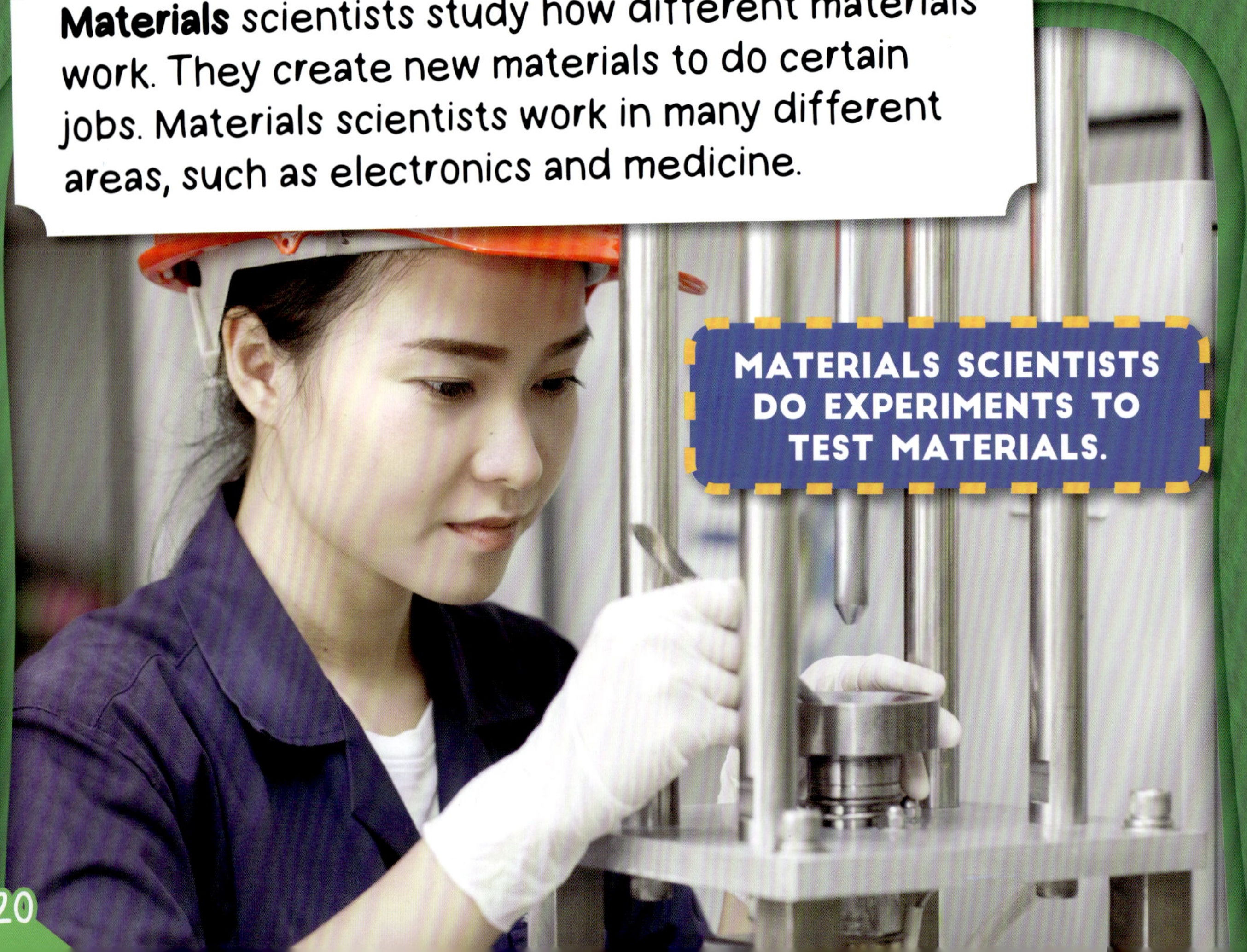

MATERIALS SCIENTISTS DO EXPERIMENTS TO TEST MATERIALS.

Different materials scientists specialize in different materials, such as metal or glass. Materials scientists need to know about chemistry and physics. They need to be thoughtful and **practical** to do their job well.

THE POWER OF STEAM

We have looked at just a few careers that use science. There are many more! Science is an amazing subject that can help the world in many different ways.

BE INSPIRED!

THINK OF ALL THE WAYS YOU COULD CHANGE THE WORLD WITH STEAM!

You could use science to do many cool things when you grow up. There are many overlapping skills in the STEAM subjects. It is important to work hard in all of them!

GLOSSARY

CAREERS	job areas that can be worked in for a large amount of a person's life
CURIOSITY	a strong wish to learn or know about things
EQUIPMENT	items that are needed to complete a certain job
EXOTIC	coming from far away, usually another country
MATERIALS	things from which objects are made
NATURAL	found in nature and not made by people
PRACTICAL	able to solve problems using knowledge and actions
SPECIALISTS	people who focus on a particular subject or skill
SURVEYS	lists of questions asked to find out particular information
THEORIES	possible explanations of how things happen

INDEX